Copyright © 2011
By Jill Cikins
First Edition

 Naampedia, LLC
100 Riverside Boulevard, Suite 6U
New York, NY 10069
naampedia.com

All rights reserved. This book is protected under the copyright laws of the United States of America. This book may not be copied or reprinted for commercial gain or profit. This book may not be reproduced in whole or in part, or by any means electronic, mechanical, photocopying, recording or other, without express written permission from the publisher, except by a reviewer, who may use a brief passage in review.

Illustration by Rosalie Peng
www.rosaliepeng.com

ISBN: 978-0-9847064-0-2

Today I am a Princess!

For the Little Princess in all of us

THIS BOOK IS DEDICATED TO *Sonia*

the most beautiful, graceful and humble Princess I am so fortunate to have in my life. Thank you for all of your guidance, support and inspiration. You have been instrumental in making this dream a reality.

ACKNOWLEDGEMENTS

This book would not have been possible without the wisdom, love and support from my teacher and mentor, Dr. Joseph Michael Levry. I thank you with all of my heart.

Many thanks to all of those who have spent time and effort helping me organize my thoughts, rhyme my words and edit my grammar; Heather, Lori, Resa, Joy, Stephanie and Rich, we are all Princes and Princesses!

To my favorite Princes' Joshua and Jonah, I love you.

Rosalie, thank you for bringing the Little Princess to life!

INTRODUCTION TO *the Little Princess*

This book was inspired in the wisdom of Universal Kabbalah, as taught by Dr. Joseph Michael Levry, which teaches that the purpose of life is to be the best we can be. With love and mastery of both esoteric sciences and the practical nature of man and the cosmos, Dr. Levry teaches that by living each day in the present and opening our eyes to the gifts and lessons that are all around us, our journey through life can truly be joyous and magical. It is my hope that the story of the Little Princess will show children of all ages that by using their imagination and focus, magical things can happen each and every day!

This is the story of a little girl who becomes a beautiful and wise princess. Along her way she meets the 7 Great Planets of the Sky as they guide her on her journey. She learns the Kabbalistic principle that each planet behaves differently in the sky and exerts a physical influence on planet Earth and on the human mind in a periodic succession equivalent to the days of the week. In this tale, magical planets speak wisdom to the little girl, provide guidance and teach an important lesson each day that brings the Little Princess closer to her Kingdom. Each planet grants our little girl a wish and a symbol to use on the day they rule as well as a magical phrase for the Little Princess to always remember.

And so begins the story of the Little Princess!

The *Sun* gives the power to be

The *Moon* gives the power to see

Mars gives the power to fight and discern

Mercury gives the power to write and to learn

Jupiter gives the power of luck and duty

Venus gives the power of balance and beauty

Unlike his brothers and sisters above,

The power of *Saturn* sets you free with love!

All of these powers you have from the start
Just look inside and live from your heart!

Each planet gives power on its own special day
and gives magical gifts to help guide the way

There is order and structure and lessons to learn
To gracefully grow with each twist and turn

So use these gifts wisely and surely you'll see
You are a great magician; be all that you can be!

Rise and shine Little Princess, a new day is here

An adventure awaits, the path is all clear!

There are seven creative planets, each one ruling a day

Chant magical phrases, and they'll show you the way.

Doors will open and beautiful Kingdoms you'll find

Awaiting a Little Princess who is wise and so kind!

I am Father Sun and I am always watching from above

Sending rays of light to all with joy and love.

I give you this crown to remind you of who you are

As you grow big and strong and become a great star!

Sing a tune, do a dance, and step onto the stage

As the butterflies you draw magically *fly* from the page!

Follow your heart Little Princess, your journey has begun

SUN

Chant:

*"Today I am a Princess,
I shine just like the Sun!"*

And so with these words the Sun sits on his Throne
And summons the other planets into his home.

SUNDAY

As the day turns to night,

Little Princess close your eyes

My Moon ball awaits to delight and surprise!

Fly high above the clouds, sprinkle pixie dust in the air

Doors to my enchanted kingdom magically appear!

I am Mother Moon and I reflect your hopes and your dreams

To show you that friendship and sharing make a Little Princess beam!

I give you this necklace to match with your gown

It grows stronger and stronger as the pearls go around.

MOON

As my reflection lights the dance floor

crickets chirp and sway

Foxes trot, bunnies hop

and hungry hippos munch at the buffet!

Use your imagination Little Princess,

to see what you can be

Chant:

"Today I am a fairy Princess,
living my dreams with glee!"

The Moon steps to the side, as Mars bursts in like fire

A brave warrior at heart, to protect is his desire.

MONDAY

Today Little Princess, your Kingdom looks up to you

Use my energy and strength to lead in all you do!

Shouts come from the village, a dragon is in town!

Flames shoot from his nose as he lurks all around.

I am Mars and I am full of vigor and might

MARS

But it's the strategy and focus

that makes a heroic knight!

I give you this sword

to protect your family and friends

Believe in yourself, and on you they can depend!

The right action takes thought, so be calm and be clever

As patience makes a Little Princess braver than ever!

A loving heart tames the dragon, a loyal friend you will see

His eternal flames warm the castle, a happy home it will be.

Do not let challenges or obstacles stop you on the way

Chant:

"Today I am a courageous Princess,
I will help save the day!"

The conflict is over, there is danger no more

Mercury races to the front, ready to explore.

TUESDAY

Hurry! Hurry! There is no time to wait

I carry big news and I cannot be late!

There is so much to write, so much to tell

So much to share and so much to sell.

I am Mercury and I am pleased to meet you,

On a brief stop from Egypt, then off to Machu Picchu!

I give you this compass to direct your path North

Where there is always a solution, and a way to go forth!

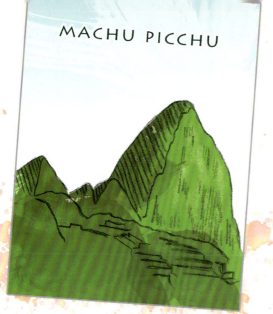

On your journey make new friends,

learn new customs and glories

Use these adventures to become wise,

teach others, and tell stories

In a journal keep good notes and write down the tale

Of how you became a princess and a sweet nightingale!

Choose your words wisely Little Princess, always speak from your heart

Chant:

"We are all connected, no matter how far apart!"

                    Mercury leaves quickly as he is always on the go

                    And Jupiter thunders in with a merry Ho! Ho! Ho!

Hip-hip-hooray Little Princess, today is your lucky day

With confidence and a leap of faith all things will go your way!

You have traveled very far and now you deserve to rest

In my grand palace with tasty food, please, come be my guest!

Like a genie in a bottle at the tip of your hand

I will grant you three wishes whenever you command!

You can use them for yourself or to help the greater good

Share new toys, feed a clan, or clean-up your neighborhood.

I am Lord Jupiter and I give you this four-leaf clover of luck

Use it wisely to serve and help those that are stuck.

When you give from your heart, you will see it's no chore

Each act of kindness comes back to you with rewards…3 times more!

You will learn, Little Princess, this wise and simple rule:

Chant:

"To give is to receive, to help others makes you cool!"

With luck on your side and your journey almost done
Venus twirls to the front with a song and a hum.

THURSDAY

Give a cheer Little Princess, let's go outside and play

A pretty dress with six red roses brings smiles to all today!

I am Venus, the goddess of beauty, the brightest star above

I help the flowers bloom with life, spreading seeds with love.

Go frolic in the forest and say hello to all the trees

Thank them for their shelter and the fresh air that we breathe.

Birds sing sweet melodies and spiders spin a web of lace

Our senses are happy when we speak and act with grace.

I give you this perfume to attract all that is sweet

And to share a bit of sweetness with everyone you meet!

VENUS

Splish-splash in the river, see a frog leap from pad to pad

Could a simple kiss turn a frog into a handsome lad?

Little Princess, look around, beauty is always in our sight

Chant:

"Today I am a beautiful Princess spreading Love, Peace and Light!"

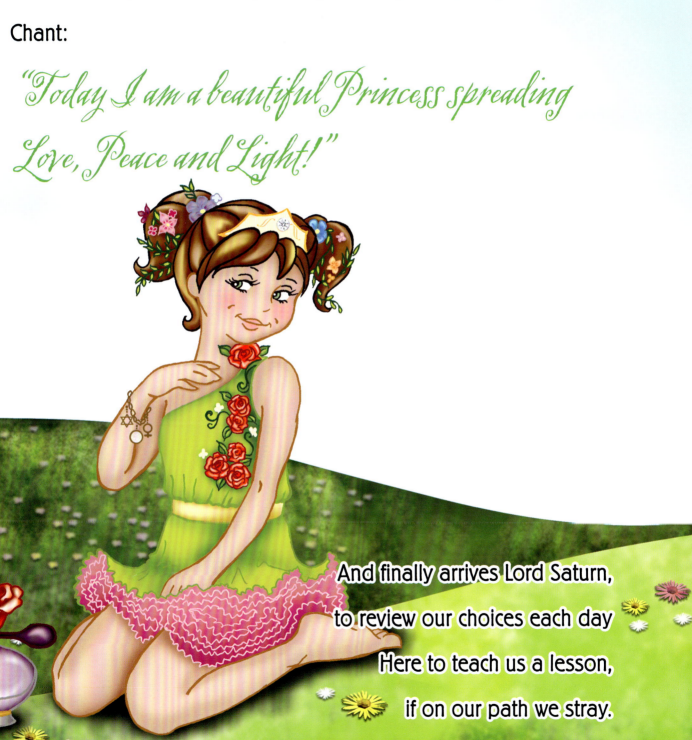

And finally arrives Lord Saturn, to review our choices each day
Here to teach us a lesson, if on our path we stray.

FRIDAY

SATURN

Once upon a time Little Princess, your were just a tiny seed

You bravely faced adventures for your journey to proceed.

I am Lord Saturn and I watch and take measure

To make sure you are deserving when I offer my treasure.

When want is too much and give is too small

I take things away and your journey may stall.

When want is in balance and you give with joy

I surely will surprise you with a wish or a toy.

I give you this ring, a symbol of completion and unity

Remember, be who you are in each and every opportunity!

This journey is now ending; did you help others in need?

If so, Little Princess, make a wish and it shall be granted indeed!

Chant:

"I am grateful and thankful to be who I am"

Chant:

"Today I am a Princess, I am, I am!"

SATURDAY

The following prayer will help you and your loved ones increase and spread your own special light.

"By reciting the prayer of light daily, you automatically become a benefactor of humankind. By projecting the words of love, peace and light you are sending out constructive healing vibrations of light to help, uplift, enlighten and heal others."
— Dr. Joseph Michael Levry

Love before me	Peace before me	Light before me
Love behind me	Peace behind me	Light behind me
Love at my left	Peace at my left	Light at my left
Love at my right	Peace at my right	Light at my right
Love above me	Peace above me	Light above me
Love below me	Peace below me	Light below me
Love unto me	Peace unto me	Light unto me
Love in my surroundings	Peace in my surroundings	Light in my surroundings
Love to all	Peace to all	Light to all
Love to the universe	Peace to the universe	Light to the universe

— Dr. Joseph Michael Levry

ABOUT THE AUTHOR

Jill is a long time student of Dr. Joseph Michael Levry and is a certified Naam Yoga Instructor and Harmonuym Practitioner. She is the founder and owner of Naampedia.com, a website dedicated to sharing the wisdom and practical tools of Naam Yoga. Jill loves to run and do any form of exercise on Tuesdays, travel on Wednesdays and make cookies for friends and family on Thursdays! She lives in the magical Kingdom of New York City tries to be the best Princess she can be, each and every day. This is her first children's book.

ABOUT THE ILLUSTRATOR

Rosalie is a professional graphic artist, illustrator and a dedicated mother of two. She is co-founder of 2 retail fashion companies. JustB Apparel, a retail apparel company that specializes in clothes with a positive message; and Lineage, a luxury retail accessories company that creates unique and custom monogram jewelry. Rosalie is an avid baker and an adventurous home cook. She is originally from New York and now resides in New Jersey.